HORSEPOWER

DUNE BUGGIES

by Jennifer L. Marks

Reading Consultant:

Barbara L. Fox

Reading Specialist

North Carolina State University

Capstone
press

Mankato, Minnesota

Blazers is published by Capstone Press,
151 Good Counsel Drive, P.O. Box 669, Mankato, Minnesota 56002.
www.capstonepress.com

Library of Congress Cataloging-in-Publication Data
Marks, Jennifer L.
    Dune buggies / by Jennifer L. Marks.
    p. cm.—(Blazers. Horsepower)
    Summary: "Simple text and photographs describe dune buggies,
their design, and uses"—Provided by publisher.
    Includes bibliographical references and index.
    ISBN-13: 978-0-7368-6447-3 (hardcover)
    ISBN-10: 0-7368-6447-4 (hardcover)
    1. Dune buggies—Juvenile literature. I. Title. II. Series.
TL236.7.M37 2007
629.222—dc22   2006001008

Editorial Credits
Sarah L. Schuette, editor; Thomas Emery and Patrick D. Dentinger,
    book designers; Jason Knudson, set designer; Jo Miller, photo
    researcher; Scott Thoms, photo editor

Photo Credits
2006 Trackside Photo, 4–5, 6, 7, 8–9, 17, 20, 22–23, 24–25, 28–29
Artemis Images, cover, 16, 18–19
Corbis/Jim Sugar, 26
Getty Images Inc./Kevin Winter, 10–11
Shutterstock/Richard C. Bennett, 21
Unicorn Stock Photos/Jim Argo, 12–13, 14, 15

**The author dedicates this book to her sister, Lisa Marks, of
Cody, Wyoming.**

TABLE OF CONTENTS

CATCHING AIR

The growl of powerful dune buggy engines fills the desert. Zipping up and down hills of sand, one daring driver aims for the biggest dune.

The buggy races up the dune.
It launches off the top and zooms
through the air. The buggy lands
with a bounce and roars off to the
next dune.

BLAZER FACT

The wind shapes sand into dunes. Sand dunes can look like ridges, mounds, and even stars.

Not even the tallest dunes can stop these speedsters. Catching air is what dune buggies do best.

Catching air

BLAZER FACT

Drivers try to avoid large dips called "witch eyes" in sand dunes. Buggies can flip if they hit them.

DESIGN

Big tires and lightweight
frames make buggies perfect
for racing across beaches
and deserts.

Many dune buggies have smooth, soft front tires. The back tires are tall and wide. Big treads, called paddles, help push buggies through sand.

Paddles

Whip

Safety is important. Roll cages
and harnesses protect drivers.
Whips help drivers spot each other
when speeding up and down hills.

Roll cage

Dune buggies hit many dips
and bumps. Shock absorbers make
the ride smoother. Skid plates
keep buggies from catching on
rough terrain.

Shock absorber

Skid plate

REV THE ENGINE

Dune buggies have powerful engines. Many buggies use engines from motorcycles or small cars.

Many dune buggies have air-cooled engines. These buggies drive so fast that the rushing air cools the engines.

BLAZER FACT

Dune buggies are so light that the engine doesn't need a lot of gas. They can get 40 miles (64 kilometers) to the gallon.

Dune Buggy Parts

Shocks

Tires

Roll cage

Skid plate

BUGGIES IN ACTION

Buggie races are held all over the United States. Fans love to watch their favorite buggies battle to the finish line.

Even the U.S. military uses dune buggies to carry spies deep into enemy land. No matter their uses, dune buggies can travel anywhere.

ONE BUCKING BUGGY!

GLOSSARY

catching air (KACH-ing AIR)—a term for when all wheels of a vehicle leave the ground

harness (HAR-niss)—the set of straps that hold a driver in place

paddles (PAD-uhlz)—the series of raised ridges across a tire

roll cage (ROHL KAYJ)—the structure of strong metal tubing that protects a dune buggy driver if a buggy rolls

shock absorber (SHOK ab-ZORB-uhr)—a part of a vehicle that lessens the shock of driving on rough surfaces

terrain (thu-RAYN)—the surface of the land

READ MORE

Budd, E. S. *Dune Buggies.* Sports Machines. Chanhassen, Minn.: Child's World, 2004.

Hale, James. *Dune Buggies.* Enthusiast Color. St. Paul, Minn.: MBI, 2004.

INTERNET SITES

FactHound offers a safe, fun way to find Internet sites related to this book. All of the sites on FactHound have been researched by our staff.

Here's how:

1. Visit *www.facthound.com*

2. Choose your grade level.

3. Type in this book ID **0736864474** for age-appropriate sites. You may also browse subjects by clicking on letters, or by clicking on pictures and words.

4. Click on the **Fetch It** button.

FactHound will fetch the best sites for you!

INDEX